Visits to Terrestria

A Guide for
Parents, Teachers, and Students

Based on the Terrestria Chronicles
by Ed Dunlop

www.TalesOfCastles.com
cover art and design by Wayne Coley

Visits to terrestria: a study guide/by Ed Dunlop
Dunlop, Ed
[Ringgold, Ga.]: *Cross and Crown Publishing*, c2007
115p.; 213cm
Terrestria chronicles study guide
Dewey Call # 813.54 ISBN 0-9785523-7-7

The answer key for this study guide is available as
a free download at www.TalesOfCastles.com.

Dunlop, Ed.
Middle ages juvenile fiction.
Christian life juvenile fiction.
Allegories.
Fantasy.

Printed and bound in the United States of America

A note to parents and teachers...

Suggestions for reading the Terrestria Chronicles series and using this study guide:

1. Pray for the working of the Holy Spirit in hearts as you read the stories. The Terrestria series was written first and foremost to honor the matchless name of our great Savior, the Lord Jesus Christ, and then to challenge the readers to love and serve Him with all their hearts. The stories are exciting and thrilling to read, but remember, each has a powerful message and a definite purpose.

2. Allow the Lord to work in your own heart as you read the story with/to your children/students. Much of the message of the series is directed to the adult reader. Recognize this and be receptive to the Holy Spirit of God as He ministers to your own heart.

3. Decide in advance if you are going to read ahead of your children/students. If you choose to read ahead, you may be better prepared to guide discussions that are sure to follow as you finish particular chapters. On the other hand, if you choose not to read ahead, you and your students can experience the wonder of discovering the stories together.

4. It is suggested that you read through a particular book in its entirety and then go back and work through the appropriate section of the study guide with your students. This will allow your young people to thoroughly enjoy the story the first time through and then revisit familiar scenes as you use the study guide to lead discussions and dig deeper into the Biblical truths presented in the series.

5. Watch for "teachable moments". As you read through the series, spontaneous questions will often arise from time to time. Do not be in such a hurry to finish a chapter that you miss these valuable opportunities to teach and re-emphasize the Biblical truths presented in the stories.

6. In your discussions, take the students back to Scripture as often as possible. Make frequent use of questions such

as: "What does the Bible say about this?" or, "Can you give a Scriptural reason for that answer?" When we put an emphasis on Biblical answers we show our young people that the Word of God is the foundation for our faith.

7. Remember that you do not have to use every question in this guide. The purpose of this study guide is to invoke discussions of the spiritual truths taught in the stories. If interest lags at a particular point, end the discussion and return to it at another time. You might want to peruse a particular section of the guide before exploring it with your children/students, deciding in advance which questions you will use.

8. Feel free to pose questions of your own. If you are in tune with the needs of your young people, the questions that you phrase may be more appropriate and better address issues that are vital to your students. Often you will want to write questions out in advance, but many times spontaneous questions will occur during a discussion.

9. Be sure to take the part of a participant, rather than just a guide. Discover together the wonder of the stories and the uplifting truths that they contain.

10. The JUST FOR FUN section at the end of each chapter has suggested activities for various age groups. While designed for fun and enjoyment, many of the activities will also reinforce the spiritual messages of the books. Do not try to do all of the activities; choose the ones that are the most appropriate for your family or for your class. (You might even let your young people help in the selection—often they will learn most from the ones that they choose.)

11. Finally, enjoy your visits to Terrestria!

Book One
The Sword, the Ring, and the Parchment

The first book in the Terrestria Chronicles tells the story of Josiah, a young slave who is freed by the King of Terrestria, Emmanuel. The story is an allegory, a story that illustrates spiritual truth, a story with a deeper meaning. *The Sword, the Ring, and the Parchment* was written to give you a sense of wonder and a sense of deep gratitude when you think of your King and your salvation.

1. In an allegory, the people, places, and events are representations or pictures of something else. In order to understand the meaning of the story, it is important that you recognize the main characters of the book. In *The Sword, the*

> **"...with Emmanuel as your Lord, your future holds delights of the soul such as you cannot imagine."**
> **–Sir Faithful**

Ring, and the Parchment, the three main characters are Argamor, King Emmanuel, and Josiah. Tell who each character represents:

Argamor _____

King Emmanuel _____

Josiah _____

2. What does the kingdom of Terrestria represent?

_____

Where do you suppose the name "Terrestria" came from and what does it mean?

_____

Author's note: Readers have asked what the name "Argamor" means. It is not taken from Scripture or from the Biblical languages; the first syllable is simply an unpleasant sound; the last syllable comes from the Latin word for "death".

3. In chapters 1-4, the author attempts to portray the hopeless condition of those who are lost without Christ. Josiah is described as a miserable, helpless slave who deplores his servitude to Argamor, the Dungeon of Condemnation, and the chain of iniquity and weight of guilt. As one might imagine, he is desperate to escape. With number one as the worst, arrange the following story elements in the order in which you think they would have affected Josiah:

_____ The Dungeon of Condemnation

_____ Servitude to Argamor

_____ The cold and rain

_____ The heat from the flaming forge

_____ Lack of food

_____ Loneliness

_____ The cruelty of Evilheart and Lawofsin

_____ The chain of iniquity and weight of guilt

_____ The backbreaking work of filling the forge

4. In chapter 3, Father Almsdeeds offered Josiah a ray of false hope when he gave the poor slave the three golden keys. Who does Father Almsdeeds represent?

_____

_____

5. Why was Josiah unable to escape by using the golden keys?

_____

6. What are some of the "golden keys" that people sometimes use

today in an attempt to free themselves from condemnation?

1. _____

2. _____

3. _____

7. The major religions of the world teach salvation by one form of works or another. Name three different religions and then tell what each teaches regarding salvation:

1. _____ : _____

2. _____ : _____

3. _____ : _____

8. What is the difference between religion and faith in Christ?

_____

_____

9. Which is the Biblical way of salvation? _____

10. Thought question: If a person is trusting in his religion or his good works for his salvation, is he trusting in Christ? _____ Is this person saved? _____

11. What part do works have in our salvation? _____

_____

Give two Scripture references to support your answer:

1. _____

2. _____

12. **Thought question:** Why do the religions of the world teach

4

salvation by works (or by adherence to that particular religion)
when the Bible clearly teaches salvation by faith in Christ
alone? _____

_____

_____

13. Place a checkmark beside the three words that you think best
describe both Argamor and Satan:

❑ Vicious ❑ Destroyer ❑ Cruel
❑ Kind ❑ Weak ❑ Helpful
❑ Powerful ❑ Cunning ❑ Caring
❑ Warlord ❑ Hateful ❑ Ignorant

14. Now list three words (or names) that the Bible uses to describe Satan (give references):
1. _____ _____
2. _____ _____
3. _____ _____

15. In Chapter 5, we see Josiah at his lowest, and yet the story
becomes glorious when King Emmanuel appears. Choose four words
or phrases from the story that best describe the King of Terrestria:

1. _____

2. _____

3. _____

4. _____

16. Give four phrases from John's description of King Jesus in
Revelation 1:13-18:

1. _____

2. _____

3. _____

4. _____

17. Write a short paragraph that describes the scene when King Emmanuel set Josiah free:

_____

_____

_____

_____

_____

18. If you have received Jesus as your Savior, you have experienced what Prince Josiah experienced. Write a short paragraph telling about the day when the King set you free and adopted you:

_____

_____

_____

_____

_____

_____

_____

19. Choose four words or phrases that best describe your King:

1. _____

2. _____

3. _____

4. _____

20. When Josiah arrived at the Castle of Faith, he found it to be

a place of peace and great joy. After reading chapters 6 and 7, arrange the following story elements in the order in which you think they would have affected Josiah, with number one as the best:

_____ The bountiful food
_____ The fellowship in the great hall
_____ The music in the great hall
_____ Sir Faithful's love and guidance
_____ The colorful banners in the great hall
_____ The constellations glorifying King Emmanuel
_____ The comfortable solar
_____ The freedom from the chain of iniquity and weight of guilt

21. In chapter 7, Josiah met Sir Preparation, the castle armorer, who outfitted him with armor. Name the various pieces of armor given to Josiah:

1. _____
2. _____
3. _____
4. _____
5. _____
6. _____

22. Which of the six did he already have? _____

23. Describe King Emmanuel's coat of arms: _____

_____

_____

24. Describe the coat of arms on the Shield of Faith given to Prince Josiah: _____

_____

_____

25. Why was there a second crown on the coat of arms, while Emmanuel's coat of arms had only one? _____
_____

26. Where in the Bible do we find the pieces of the "armor of God" listed? _____

27. Can you name them? (Try it first without looking at the Bible passage.)

1. _____
2. _____
3. _____
4. _____
5. _____
6. _____

28. Prince Josiah asked, "Why am I being equipped for battle?" What was Sir Faithful's answer?_____
_____
_____

29. What is the "Great War" of which the castle steward spoke? (Hint: It is far more than just good against evil.) _____
_____
_____

30. Where in Scripture are we told of this war? _____
_____
_____

31. Who is our enemy? _____

32. **Thought question:** What are you doing to protect yourself against this enemy?_____

_____

_____

33. Which piece of armor did Sir Preparation say was the most important? _____

_____

34. Why did he say this?_____

_____

_____

35. Which piece of armor does Ephesians 6 say is the most important? _____

36. When Josiah asked for a sword, what did Sir Preparation give him? _____

37. Describe the book and tell what it could do:_____

_____

_____

_____

38. Josiah's book, of course, is a representation of the Bible. Why does the author portray it as capable of becoming a sword?

_____

_____

_____

39. As you view our society, what events do you see that give evidence to the fact that the Great War is raging today?_____

_____

_____

40. What weapons are being used today by our enemy to destroy lives and families? Check all that apply:

❏ Television
❏ Popular music
❏ Peer pressure
❏ Educational system
❏ Public libraries
❏ Recreational activities
❏ Worldly philosophies
❏ Materialism (desire for wealth and possessions)
❏ Other _____

41. In chapter 8, Prince Josiah asked to be immersed in the Sea of Conviction to show that he was following King Emmanuel. What Biblical ordinance does this represent? _____

42. According to Romans 6:3-5, what does baptism symbolize?

_____

43. Sometimes different forms of baptism are practiced: sprinkling, pouring, immersion, etc. If baptism symbolizes the death, burial, and resurrection of the Lord Jesus, which form of baptism would present a complete picture? _____

44. Describe the petitions as presented by Sir Faithful in chapter 8:

_____

_____

45. **Thought question:** If you are a child of the King, how often do you make use of your right to send petitions to the King?

46. In chapter 8, why did Sir Faithful ask Josiah to wash his feet? Check all that apply:
❑   The steward was old and had a hard time reaching his own feet.
❑   Josiah was beginning to develop a haughty attitude.
❑   Sir Faithful wanted to teach Josiah about servanthood.
❑   King Emmanuel had once washed the feet of his followers.

47. Sir Faithful told Josiah, "You were saved to be _____ _____."

48. Finish this quote from Sir Faithful: "Your chief goal in life should be to _____ _____ _____."

49. In chapter 9, Prince Thomas is presented as being an arrogant, boastful young man. What do you think was Thomas' problem? What had he forgotten?

_____
_____
_____

50. Why was Thomas not effective with his sword?

_____
_____
_____

51. In chapter 10, Lord Watchful taught Prince Josiah the three duties of a sentry. What are they?
1. _____
2. _____
3. _____

52. How would we guard our castle (heart) in these three same ways?

1. _____

2. _____

3. _____

53. In chapter 12, you met two unusual characters known as Palaois Anthropos and Neos Anthropos. In your own words, tell who these two men represent:

    Palaois: _____

    Neos: _____

54. In chapter 14, Prince Josiah was given the task of delivering an important parchment to the Castle of Unity, yet he failed in the assignment. Why did he fail?

_____

_____

55. Name three things (perhaps even *good* things) that often keep people today from serving their King:

1. _____

2. _____

3. _____

56. What did Prince Josiah lose as a result of his failure? Put a check mark beside the things that he lost and an X beside the ones he only thought he had lost.

    ❑ His joy
    ❑ His position as a son of King Emmanuel
    ❑ His right to send petitions
    ❑ His right to serve the King
    ❑ His effectiveness in serving the King
    ❑ His freedom from the weight of guilt

57. Briefly describe his liberation from the Dungeon of Condemnation (the second time):

_____

_____

_____

_____

_____

_____

58. In Chapter 17, after Josiah had been set free from the dungeon, Encouragement showed him a stream and instructed him to wade into it to cleanse his garments. Of what Scripture verse does this scene remind you?

_____

59. Before leaving Josiah, Encouragement warned the young prince of the Giant of Fear, yet the giant captured him easily. Why?

_____

_____

60. What fears do people sometimes face in regards to their salvation and their position as a child of the King?

_____

_____

_____

61. Are these fears based on fact? _____ Give Scripture references to support your answer:

_____

_____

_____

62. What enabled Prince Josiah to escape the Giant of Fear and the Castle of Unbelief?

_____

_____

_____

63. The prince worried about the reception he would receive at the Castle of Faith. How was he received at the castle and what did he learn?

_____

_____

_____

_____

64. Imagine that *you* are sending a petition of gratitude to *your* King for setting you free and adopting you into His family. What would you say?

_____

_____

_____

_____

_____

65. What was the greatest truth that you found illustrated in *The Sword, the Ring, and the Parchment?*

_____

_____

_____

_____

66. What was your favorite part of the book?

_____

_____

_____

_____

_____

_____

For further study: John 3:1-18; John 5:24; Rom. 10:8-15; Eph. 1:3-23; Eph. 2:4-10; I John 3:1-5; I John 5:11-15; I John 1:5-10

MEMORIZE: Romans 8:15-17

JUST FOR FUN!*

1. Choose a particular chapter (or scene) from the book and act it out with your class or with your family.

2. Make a parchment from King Emmanuel proclaiming you as His child. The wording for your parchment can be found on page 42 of the *Sword, the Ring, and the Parchment*. If you can do calligraphy, use this to make the document as attractive as possible. Frame the parchment and hang it in your bedroom as a reminder that you are a child of the King.

3. Make a Helmet of Salvation from papier-mâché. Can you design a moving face shield that can be raised and lowered?

4. Make a map of the various places visited in the book. Draw some of the places.

5. Make fabric banners of the constellations mentioned in the book. Hang them in your classroom or family room as reminders that King Emmanuel is Lord of all. (If fabric is unavailable or too expensive, draw the banners on paper.)

6. Cook a fancy meal representative of the one from the great hall.

7. Create a Petition Book and remember to send petitions (pray) throughout the day.

8. Draw a castle or make a model of one from construction paper or papier-mâché.

*Special thanks to Kris Price www.homeschoolblogger.com/classicaleducation4me) for providing many of the creative, fun ideas in this study guide.

Book Two

The Quest for Seven Castles

The second book of the Terrestria series is based on II Peter 1:5-8 and emphasizes the need for growth in the Christian life. God desires that we grow to become like His Son, the Lord Jesus. In the

> **"Lift your voice in praise to King Emmanuel, and the Swamp of Bitterness will lose its power over you."**
> **–Lord Thankful**

story of Prince Josiah's quest to the seven castles of Terrestria, the ultimate goal was that he would grow to be like King Emmanuel.

1. As we begin this study, list the names of the seven castles in the order in which Prince Josiah visited them, and then draw a line from each castle to the jewel that he obtained at that castle:

Castle of _____	Diamond
Castle of _____	Amethyst
Castle of _____	Sapphire
Castle of _____	Fire opal
Castle of _____	Ruby
Castle of _____ _____	Unnamed
Castle of _____	Emerald

2. You'll notice that the seventh jewel is not named. What do you think it should be? _____

3. When Josiah begged Sir Faithful to accompany him on the quest, the castle steward told the young prince that he would receive guidance from two sources. Without looking in the book, name the two sources: the _____ and the _____.

4. Remembering that the story is an allegory and that the characters and events in the story represent something or someone else, what do these two sources of guidance represent in our lives as we seek to become like Jesus? _____ and
_____.

5. In *The Quest for Seven Castles*, Prince Josiah had to overcome at least one obstacle to reach each particular castle. What was the first obstacle he had to overcome to reach the Castle of Virtue?

_____

_____

6. When Josiah first met Envy, the Littlekin was barely ten inches high, yet as the young prince prepared to wrestle him, he became a hulking giant of a man. What Biblical truth do you suppose the author is trying to portray in this scene?

_____

_____

_____

7. Sir Wisdom told Josiah that he would face three tests of his integrity. What were they? Put a check mark beside the one(s) that Josiah passed.

❏ _____
❏ _____
❏ _____

8. While Josiah was at the Castle of Virtue, Sir Honorable taught him that he had no virtue of his own. According to Sir Honorable, where does true virtue come from?

_____

_____

9. What did he tell Josiah to do to acquire virtue?

_____

_____

10. What was Sir Faithful's definition of *virtue*? (Hint: his definition can be found in *Strong's Concordance.*)

_____

_____

11. In Chapter 7, on the journey to the Castle of Knowledge, Josiah met and conquered thirteen dark knights. Why did the dark knights conquer him when they attacked a second time?

_____

_____

_____

12. What gave Prince Josiah the courage to attack the dark knights at the campfire in order to recover his sword?

_____

Why was he victorious?

_____

13. In Chapter 8, Josiah accepted a carriage ride from a man named Skeptic. Cross out each description that does ***not*** apply to Skeptic.

Well-dressed
Well-educated
Rich merchant   Deceitful
Smooth talking   Truthful
Confused   Agent for Argamor
Loyal to Emmanuel   Intelligent
                                Backward
                                Illiterate

14. List three things that Skeptic told Prince Josiah about truth:

1. _____

2. _____

3. _____

15. Skeptic's arguments contained just enough truth to sound convincing, and Josiah was confused as a result. Name one true statement and one false statement that Skeptic made:

True: _____

False: _____

16. In what ways does Satan try to make us doubt God's Word?

_____

_____

_____

_____

17. Describe the Desert of Doubt:

_____

_____

_____

_____

18. Can you think of a situation when something (or someone) caused you to doubt God's Word or God's promises? Tell about it:

_____

_____

_____

_____

_____

19. Who rescued Prince Josiah from the Desert of Doubt?

_____

20. Describe the Castle of Knowledge:

_____

_____

_____

21. Describe the Library of Learning:

_____

_____

_____

22. Why do you suppose the author presents each book in the library as an enormous painting?

_____

_____

_____

23. What was the purpose of the library?

_____

_____

_____

24. In what way was the last volume in the library different from all the others?

_____

_____

_____

25. Why was Josiah so reluctant to leave the Castle of Knowledge?

_____

_____

_____

26. In Chapter 11, the stubborn horse (Ego) is a picture of what?

_____

27. Why did Josiah have so much trouble controlling him?

_____

_____

_____

28. Where did he end up as a result of his self-consciousness and self-pity?

_____

29. What was the only means of escape from the swamp?

_____

30. Name two things that happen when we praise God:

1. _____

2. _____

31. Give two Scriptural references that command us to praise the Lord:

1. _____

2. _____

32. What was Woebegone's real name? _____.

Who sent him to accompany Josiah through the Mountains of

Difficulty?

_____

33. During their trek through the Mountains of Difficulty, at night-fall the two travelers always found a cabin prepared for them in just the right location. What is the author trying to portray?

_____

34. How did Woebegone lure Josiah from the Path of Righteous-ness? _____

What was the result? _____

35. Name two things that Josiah tried in his attempts to escape from the Valley of Discouragement:
1. _____
2. _____

36. What was the only way of escape?

_____

_____

37. In Chapter 12, a temptress named Prosperity tempted Prince Josiah. What device did she use to do it?

_____

What does this device represent?

_____

What temptation did she place before him?

_____

38. According to Contentment, when do possessions become dangerous?

_____

_____

39. Why do possessions sometimes become more important to us than service to our King?

_____

_____

_____

40. Contentment told Josiah that it is wrong for a man to _____ in his riches more than he _____ in his King, and _____ his riches more than he _____ his King.

41. How can you guard your own heart against the deceitfulness of riches as mentioned in Matthew 13:22?

_____

_____

_____

42. After getting victory over Prosperity and her temptations of Worldly Wealth, Josiah found himself facing twelve huge adversaries in the Vale of Giants. Name them:

1._____   7. _____

2._____   8._____

3._____   9._____

4._____   10._____

5._____   11._____

6._____   12._____

43. What significance do you find in the fact that Prince Josiah faced the temptations of Worldly Wealth and evil giants while he was on his way to the Castle of Godliness?

_____

_____

_____

_____

44. What two things did Josiah do that were key to his complete victory over the giants?

1. _____

2. _____

45. Imagine that *you* have just found yourself facing twelve huge adversaries in the Vale of Giants and that you are sending a desperate petition to *your* King. What would you say?

_____

_____

_____

_____

_____

_____

_____

46. In Chapter 17, Josiah passed through the City of Wounded Hearts and was treated very unkindly by several of the residents of the city. Name three of these people:

1. _____

2. _____

3. _____

47. Sir Compassion enabled Josiah to see the hearts of the unkind people of the city, and thus he saw why they responded as they did. What burden was borne by each of the following?

The peasant farmer: _____

_____

The heavyset woman: _____

_____

The spice merchant: _____

_____

48. What valuable lesson did Josiah learn in the City of Wounded Hearts?

_____

_____

49. In Chapter 18, Josiah found himself battling a fearsome adversary determined to keep him from reaching the Castle of Charity. What was this adversary?

_____

_____

_____

50. What was Sir Compassion's definition of the word *charity*?

_____

_____

51. Who was the prince that Josiah met and what had happened to him?

_____

_____

_____

52. Why did Josiah find it so hard to sacrifice the diamond to help Prince Selwyn?

_____

_____

_____

53. What did he gain by giving up the diamond?

_____

_____

54. How did Prince Josiah get another diamond?
   ❑ He earned it by going on another quest.
   ❑ His diamond was replaced by Sir Agape.
   ❑ He never did get another diamond.
   ❑ He recovered his diamond from the coachman.

55. What happened to Prince Josiah and Prince Selwyn on the third day of their stay at the Castle of Charity?

_____

_____

56. What was King Emmanuel's purpose in sending Josiah (and also, Selwyn) on the quest for the seven castles?

_____

_____

For further study: I Peter 3:18; Galatians 3:1-29; Phil. 4:8; I John 4:7-13; I Cor. 13; I Cor. 9:25-27; Psalm 37:7-9; Psalm 146-150

MEMORIZE: II Peter 1:5-8

JUST FOR FUN!

1. Create a shield with fake gems from a craft store. As you read *The Quest for Seven Castles*, glue the appropriate jewel to the shield each time Prince Josiah reaches the next castle.

2. If jewels are not available, draw the Shield of Faith and 7 jewels. Cut out the jewels and paste them to the shield.

3. Draw a map of the journey to the seven castles.

4. Make a 3-D tabletop diorama of the journey. Have seven students each make a 3-D model castle (one of the seven in the story); then use them to create a 3-D diorama of the journey, including mountains, swamps, villages, etc.

5. Draw the Library of Learning.

6. Make a 3-D model of the Library. Have each person draw one or more of the paintings (each represents a book from the Bible) and then paste them on the library walls.

7. Write a story about a journey into one of the pictures. Can you imagine a Bible story taking place in a medieval setting?

Book Three
The Search for Everyman

This third book in the Terrestria Chronicles tells of Prince Josiah's first real mission for King Emmanuel and also fully introduces the other two main characters in the series: Prince Selwyn and his sister, Princess Gilda. The book emphasizes the need to tell others of our great King and Savior, the Lord Jesus Christ.

1. *The Search for Everyman* opens with Prince Josiah in the middle of what kind of an adventure?

_____

Do you think that you would like to experience this?

_____

2. Which of the following are true about Prince Selwyn?
- ❏ He was blond.
- ❏ He was two years younger than Josiah.
- ❏ He was Gilda's older brother.
- ❏ He looked to Josiah for leadership.
- ❏ He loved King Emmanuel.
- ❏ He was fearful and afraid.
- ❏ He was jealous of Josiah.
- ❏ He was good with a sword.

3. Name three things that you know about Princess Gilda:

1. _____

2. _____

3. _____

4. In Chapter 1, King Emmanuel sent Prince Josiah, Prince Selwyn, and Princess Gilda on a quest to do what?

❑ Deliver a pardon to a condemned man.
❑ Help defend a castle against an attack.
❑ Deliver a parchment to another castle.
❑ Find an enchanted ring that was missing.

5. What was the first reaction of the three young people to the King's mission? Mark all that apply.

❑ Disappointment
❑ Excitement
❑ Fear
❑ Apathy
❑ Pride

> **"...when one steps out in faith and obedience to the King, the obstacles become small and insignificant."**
> **–Sir Wisdom**

6. To what land did Sir Faithful send them in their search?

_____

7. What three fears did Josiah express to Sir Faithful?

"What if we _____ _____ _____?"
"What if we _____ _____ _____ _____?"
"What if he _____ _____ _____ _____?"

8. Sir Faithful reassured the three young people by telling them that King Emmanuel had not given them the spirit of fear, but of power, of love, and of a sound mind. From what Scripture verse was this taken?

_____

9. What was the name of the ship that carried them on the first leg of their journey?

❑ The Good Ship Hope
❑ Fellowship
❑ Obedience
❑ The Dawn Treader

10. In four words, describe an avral: _____,

_____, _____, _____.

11. How did the avral Leidra help Gilda, Selwyn, and Josiah on their quest?

_____

_____

12. What was the name of the giant they encountered?

_____

13. Josiah and his friends were sent by King Emmanuel to deliver a pardon to a condemned man. What has our King commissioned us to do?

_____

_____

_____

14. Do we ever face the same giant when we seek to witness for our King? _____ Why do you suppose that this happens?

_____

_____

_____

_____

15. In Chapter 4, what two things did Sir Wisdom use to kill the giant?

_____and _____.

16. While attempting to take the King's pardon to the Land of Unbelief, the three emissaries had to cross what river?

_____

17. The river appeared at first to be a raging torrent at the bottom of an enormous chasm, yet when they stepped across it in faith, it turned out to be a tiny rivulet. What is being portrayed here?
- ❑ The difficulties in serving the King often appear greater than they are.
- ❑ The Land of Unbelief was facing a drought.
- ❑ A messenger from the King will face obstacles.
- ❑ Faith will overcome any obstacle to service.

18. In Chapter 6 the three travelers faced the Miasma of Lethargy. Describe it:

_____

_____

_____

19. What did it do to them?

_____

_____

_____

_____

20. Who was the mysterious singer?

_____

21. After they left the swamp, the peasant farmer told them that no one would receive the King's pardon from them since they were so muddy and their garments were soiled. Was he correct?

_____

22. Why was it so important that their garments be clean?
- ❑ Muddy clothes would make it hard for them to walk.
- ❑ Muddy clothes would be uncomfortable.
- ❑ Muddy clothes don't properly represent King Emmanuel.
- ❑ Muddy clothes really didn't matter.

23. What is the author attempting to portray in the scene with the muddy clothes?

_____

_____

_____

24. What does the Stream of Forgiveness represent?

_____

_____

_____

25. In Chapter 7, Josiah and his two companions were delayed for a period of time. What delayed them?

_____

_____

26. Who was behind the plan to build a useless bridge?

_____

27. Why did he want the three delayed?

_____

_____

28. Does the devil ever do things to keep us from delivering the King's pardon to a condemned person? _____ What does he use to keep us from witnessing?

_____

_____

_____

_____

29. In Chapter 8, as Josiah and Selwyn battled the dark knights, they were victorious at first and were defeating the enemy. Before long, however, things changed, and the enemy knights were defeating them. Why?

_____

_____

30. At last they were victorious. Why?

_____

_____

_____

31. In Chapter 9, led by Everyman's wife, Gilda, Selwyn, and Josiah went to the Dungeon of Condemnation where Everyman was imprisoned. What does the dungeon represent?

_____

_____

32. Captain Exclusion told them that the sentence of death had been passed upon every prisoner in the dungeon. What is that "sentence of death?" (Romans 5:12)

_____

_____

33. Captain Exclusion also told them that the pardon was not for Nathaniel Everyman. Was he correct? _____

34. What did Sir Wisdom tell them about the King's pardon?

_____

_____

_____

34

35. Was Sir Wisdom correct? _____ Give Scripture references to support your answer:

_____

_____

_____

36. Why did he say that little Matilda (Everyman's daughter) was safe?

_____

_____

_____

37. In Chapter 12, why did the old ferryman keep putting them off when they wanted to cross the river to the Island of Procrastination?

_____

_____

_____

38. What was his name? _____

39. In what ways were Delay and Diversion alike?
- ❑ Both worked for Argamor.
- ❑ Both were helpful.
- ❑ Both were determined to keep the pardon from Everyman.
- ❑ Neither realized that they were hindering an important mission.

40. In Chapter 13, the trio reached the island in an amazing way. Describe it:

_____

_____

_____

41. What do you think lepidopteras represent in real life?

_____

_____

42. In Chapter 14, Selwyn suggested that they dress in the uniforms of Argamor's knights to get past the guards in the Castle of Resistance. Why did Josiah insist that it

> **"I simply cannot wear the uniform of the enemy. I'm a child of the King."**
> **–Prince Josiah**

would be wrong to wear the uniform of Argamor's men? Was he right?

_____

_____

_____

_____

43. As the trio made their way through the castle corridors, they came to a vast treasure vault known as the "Chamber of Temporal Possessions and Pleasures." What does the word *temporal* mean?

❏ Valuable
❏ Costly
❏ Temporary
❏ Vanishing

44. What was the real purpose of the Chamber of Temporal Possessions and Pleasures?

_____

_____

_____

36

45. In Chapter 15, one iron door after another blocked their way. What were the names of the first four doors?

"Fear of _____"

"Fear of _____"

"Fear of _____ _____ _____ _____"

"Fear of _____"

46. What was used to open each door?

_____

_____

47. Describe Adam Everyman in just four words:

1. _____

2. _____

3. _____

4. _____

48. What was his response when Josiah, Gilda, and Selwyn offered him the King's pardon?

❑ Great joy

❑ Confusion

❑ Rejection of the pardon

❑ Weeping

49. How did the three emissaries get back out of the castle and off the island?

_____

_____

_____

_____

50. After Adam Everyman rejected the pardon a second time, what did Sir Wisdom tell the three? Check all that apply:

❑ Everyman would be given another chance.
❑ The wrong choice was Everyman's responsibility, not theirs.
❑ They had obeyed their king, therefore their mission was a success.
❑ In rejecting the pardon, Everyman had chosen death.

51. *The Search for Everyman* closes with Princess Gilda, Prince Josiah, and Prince Selwyn making plans to do what?

_____

_____

52. Imagine that *you* are sending a petition to *your* King, asking Him to help you deliver a pardon to a friend who is condemned to die. What would you say?

_____

_____

_____

_____

_____

_____

_____

For further study: Acts 1:8; Acts 8:4; Matt. 28:19, 20; Mark 16:15

MEMORIZE: Proverbs 24:11,12

JUST FOR FUN!

1. Choose a particular chapter (or scene) from the book and act it out with your class or with your family.

2. Make puppets of Josiah, Gilda, and Selwyn and create a puppet show of one of their adventures.

3. Write words to the song sung by the mysterious voice (p. 52-55). What would the temptress have sung?

4. Make a lepidoptera from colored paper, foil, colored acetate, etc.

5. Make a 3-D model or diorama of the Dungeon of Condemnation and the gallows behind it.

6. Make a 3-D model of the Island of Procrastination and the Castle of Resistance. Using the model, act out the scenes from the book with figures made from pipe cleaners.

Book Four
The Crown of Kuros

This fourth book, the very heart of the Terrestria Chronicles allegory series, will challenge you to yield your heart to your King. When the Crown of Kuros was stolen from the keep at the Castle of Faith, Prince Josiah set out on a quest to recover the crown for Emmanuel and thus be able to yield his own heart to his King. *Kuros* is a New Testament Greek word meaning "supremacy" or "lordship." In yielding the Crown of *Kuros*, Josiah yielded the lordship of his heart to Emmanuel.

1. Book Four opens with an archery tournament at the Castle of Faith. Who won the tournament?
   ❑ Sir Constant
   ❑ Sir Humility
   ❑ Sir Pretentious
   ❑ Sir Peaceable

2. What was kept in the castle keep? Put a check mark beside each item found there and a second check mark beside the most important item.
   ❑ Chests of golden coins
   ❑ Rubies, diamonds, and emeralds
   ❑ Important records of the kingdom
   ❑ Defensive weaponry
   ❑ The Crown of Kuros
   ❑ Diagrams of the castle
   ❑ Emergency food

3. Who stole the Crown of Kuros?

_____

4. What happened that allowed her to steal it?

_____

_____

_____

5. A knight at a nearby table told Josiah that the Crown of Kuros was a token of Emmanuel's right to _____ _____.
Was he correct?_____

6. What did the Crown of Kuros actually symbolize?

_____

_____

7. The minstrel, Wanderer, had the opportunity to see Morphina's power firsthand when she entered the great hall where he was performing. What did she have the power to do?

_____

_____

8. What human weakness does the character Morphina portray?
Our own _____

9. If this evil enchantress symbolizes that weakness, why do you suppose the author gave her the ability to take many forms?

_____

_____

_____

Author's note: The name "Morphina" is not taken from Scripture or from the Biblical languages. The prefix, "Morph", simply means "to change."

10. What was Prince Josiah's motivation in setting out on the quest to recover the crown for King Emmanuel?

> **"Emmanuel's throne is secure, my prince, and he will reign forever."**
> **–Sir Wisdom**

_____

_____

_____

11. How does this show that his heart was not surrendered?

_____

_____

12. What would have been the proper motivation?

_____

_____

13. Why did Sir Dedication win in the jousts against the mysterious dark knights when Prince Josiah and Prince Selwyn failed?
- ❏ He was older and more experienced.
- ❏ He was stronger than he looked.
- ❏ His heart was surrendered to his King.
- ❏ He was using a secret weapon they did not have.

14. What was the legend of the Lake of Destiny?

_____

_____

15. In the darkness of the night, Josiah had a special visitor at the campfire. Who was she, and what was her purpose in coming?

_____

_____

16. Why did she ask Josiah to walk into the lake?

_____

_____

17. In Chapter 6, as Josiah visits the Lake of Destiny, he meets a cranky old hermit. Why was the old man so cross and so fearful?

_____

_____

18. In reality, who was the old hermit?

_____

19. What did Josiah learn by visiting the lake the first time?

_____

_____

20. In Chapter 7, Josiah visited the Lake of Destiny a second time. Describe what he saw.

_____

_____

_____

_____

21. Who was the generous, happy prince that he saw?

_____

22. What was the difference between the first visit and the second?

_____

_____

_____

23. Josiah told Lady Prudence, "It is as if there are two parts to me—one part would yield completely while one part wants to be selfish and unyielded!" What Scripture(s) would describe this conflict?

_____

_____

24. In the second visit to the lake, Josiah found himself standing before the King with a pile of glittering treasure to offer. What was the source of his treasure?

_____

_____

25. What did Lady Prudence tell Josiah that he must do to hear "Well done" when he stood before the King?

_____

_____

26. What Scripture describes the day when we stand before our King to have our deeds examined (judged)?

_____

27. In Chapter 8, Josiah wondered if he really had visited the lake. What evidence did he find that proved that he had?

_____

_____

_____

28. After Prince Josiah and Prince Selwyn had searched a certain city for Morphina and the crown, Prince Josiah was approached by a person who looked like Sir Faithful, but was not really Sir Faithful. Who was it? _____

What was her purpose in impersonating the castle steward?

_____

_____

29. Why did she have Josiah climb down into a deep pit to recover the crown?

_____

_____

30. After falling into the pit, Josiah found himself in an underground cavern. How did he get out?

_____

_____

31. In Chapter 9, Selwyn and Josiah blundered into an underground city, Lower Terrestria. What monumental event was about to take place within the city?

- ❑ The residents were preparing to celebrate the city's centennial.
- ❑ Argamor was holding a council of war.
- ❑ Argamor was introducing a new weapon he had just developed.
- ❑ The dark knights were celebrating the capture of one of Emmanuel's castles.

32. Argamor told his forces that they would not win the kingdom by storming the King's castles and attacking his armies. How then did he propose to take the kingdom?

_____

_____

_____

_____

33. At the council of war, the Council of Six presented their strategies for taking the kingdom from Emmanuel. Name the six captains on the Council of Six:

Captain _____

Captain _____

Captain _____

Captain _____

Captain _____

Captain _____

34. What two devices did Captain Pleasure plan to use to spread Argamor's message across the kingdom and thus change the hearts of King Emmanuel's followers? _____ and _____

35. Was Argamor correct in saying that Emmanuel's followers could be deceived into accepting the two evil devices? _____ How would it be done?

_____

_____

36. Undoubtedly you recognize what two devices the author is portraying here. How has the devil used these to turn the hearts of believers away from the Lord?

_____

_____

37. Do you ever find yourself watching wrong things on your "spellavision"? _____

38. How much time do you spend watching television in an average week? _____ hours

39. Have you ever kept a TV viewing log? _____ (You might be surprised at how much time you actually spend. In the average American home, the TV is on for 7 hours and 7 min-utes a day; in the typical Christian home, the daily average is half an hour less. The personal average is 4½ hours daily.)

> "...we shall wrest the kingdom from the hand of Emmanuel by stealing the hearts of the King's subjects."
> –Argamor

40. How can you guard your heart against these two (and other) evil influences?

_____

_____

_____

41. Describe the coat of arms on Captain Discontent's shield:

_____

_____

_____

_____

42. What is the significance of the symbol?

_____

_____

43. What was Captain Discontent's strategy for helping Argamor overthrow Emmanuel's kingdom?

_____

_____

_____

_____

44. Our King has decreed that the ladies of the kingdom are to have a meek and quiet spirit, and that they are to be in subjection to their husbands. (I Peter 3) In what ways does our society encourage women to be just the opposite: bold, aggressive, and domineering?

_____

_____

_____

45. **Thought question:** Whose responsibility is it to teach young ladies to have a meek and quiet spirit?

_____

_____

46. In what ways did Captain Covetous describe Emmanuel's followers? Put a check mark beside all that apply:
- ❑ They can be tempted with promises of wealth.
- ❑ They have a fondness for riches.
- ❑ They become attached to their possessions.
- ❑ They judge a man's worth by his wealth and possessions.
- ❑ They are easily satisfied with the essentials of life.
- ❑ They are usually extremely grateful for what they possess.
- ❑ They have an undying passion to accumulate wealth.

47. Now go back and place a capital "M" (for me) beside each statement that describes you.

48. What device was the captain planning to use to spread the message of greed and discontent?

_____

_____

49. What was Captain Confusion's strategy to steal the hearts of King Emmanuel's followers?
- ❑ Intimidate them with a show of power.
- ❑ Tell them that the King was losing the battle for the kingdom.
- ❑ Keep them too busy to serve their King.
- ❑ Crowd their schedules with innocent but worthless activities.

50. The evil captain mentioned one diversion in particular. What was it?

_____

51. As you view the use of sports in our country today, how would you rate their use? On the scale below, place an X to indicate how you think sports are usually used.

Glorify the King ❑ ❑ ❑ ❑ ❑ ❑ ❑ ❑ ❑ Distract the people

52. How did Captain Confusion plan to use the spellavision?

_____

_____

53. How can an increase in riches and possessions draw a man's heart away from his King?

_____

_____

54. Describe the strategy of Captain Despair:

_____

_____

55. Describe the strategy of Captain Apathy:

_____

_____

56. After reading the strategies that Argamor and the Council of Six were planning to use to capture the hearts of Emmanuel's followers, can you think of any other strategies that the devil is using today to draw believers away from their Lord?

_____

_____

_____

57. **Thought question:** What are you doing to guard your heart against the devil's strategies and attacks on your mind and your heart?

_____

_____

_____

58. What scripture passages instruct us as to how to guard our hearts against Satan and his evil forces?

_____

_____

_____

59. In Chapter 14, Prince Josiah and Prince Selwyn met Sir Wisdom at a campfire. Josiah voiced a concern that had been troubling him. Finish this statement of Josiah's: "What if Argamor is able to

_____ _____ _____ _____?"

60. Sir Wisdom answered Josiah's question with a very graphic object lesson using an acorn. Describe how the old nobleman used the acorn to illustrate King Emmanuel's power:

_____

_____

_____

50

61. In the acorn illustration, Sir Wisdom compared the King to what?

_____

_____

_____

> **"Possession of the Crown of Kuros determines who will reign in the heart of one person."** – Sir Wisdom

62. He compared Argamor to what?

_____

_____

63. Josiah was still under the impression that possession of the Crown of Kuros determined who would rule over Terrestria. What did the noblemen tell him? Put a check mark beside all that apply.
- ❏ King Emmanuel would always rule Terrestria.
- ❏ The Crown of Kuros signified dominion over one heart.
- ❏ If Argamor gained possession of the crown, he would rule Terrestria.
- ❏ Only one person could return the crown to King Emmanuel.

64. In Chapter 15, Josiah remembered something that he had witnessed in the Lake of Destiny and he determined to return the Crown of Kuros to the King in order to surrender his own heart. What event did he recall?

_____

_____

_____

65. Lady Prudence met Josiah at the campfire and told him that the crown was in the possession of what creature?

_____

_____

66. What does the name "Authades" mean? (Hint: Look in Strong's Concordance, Greek Dictionary entry #829.)

_____ or _____

67. Where did Josiah have to go to find the silver parchments?

_____

_____

68. As Josiah talked with Lady Prudence at the campfire, he abruptly reached a conclusion and made a life-changing decision. What was that decision? He would _____
in order to _____.

69. As Josiah set out to destroy the dragon, he was met by Morphina, impersonating Lady Prudence. What did she tell him NOT to do?

_____

_____

70. Why did she tell him not to do this?

_____

_____

71. Josiah was then met by what group of people that he had also encountered on his quest for the seven castles?

_____

72. What did these people try to do?

_____

73. How can "little sins" keep us from surrendering our hearts to the Lord?

_____

_____

74. Josiah then met what person who attempted to dissuade him from battling the dragon?
- ❑ A wounded knight
- ❑ A beautiful princess
- ❑ Sir Faithful
- ❑ Another young prince

75. As Josiah battled the person who sought to turn him aside, he realized who it was. Who was this person? _____

Why did this person seek to dissuade him from battling Authades the dragon?

_____

_____

76. Name some things that often keep us from surrendering our "Crown of Kuros" to our King:

_____

_____

77. In Chapter 18, following the instructions from the silver scroll—The Book of Memory—Josiah sowed the golden seed. Upon what four types of soil did it fall? _____, _____, _____, and _____.

78. What did the grain from the harvest typify?

_____

_____

79. What did Josiah learn as a result of planting the seed?

_____

_____

_____

80. In Chapter 19, Josiah faced the dragon Authades in order to recover the Crown of Kuros for King Emmanuel. Remembering the meaning of the dragon's name, what was the young prince actually battling in order to surrender the crown and his heart to the King?

_____

_____

_____

81. Inside the dragon's lair Josiah made a gruesome discovery that told him that other knights had not been victorious against Authades. What did he discover?

_____

_____

_____

82. Describe the dragon:

_____

_____

_____

83. After Josiah wounded the dragon, what did Authades offer him in exchange for the crown?

_____

_____

_____

84. When Josiah rejected the offer, what did the dragon offer him in exchange for his life?

_____

_____

_____

85. As Josiah persisted in his plan to destroy the dragon, Authades told him, "I warn you, insolent prince, that in wounding me, you wound yourself. My pain will be your pain. Should you prevail and somehow slay me, you would slay a part of yourself. Do you still desire to destroy me, knowing that it will cost you?" What did the dragon mean?

_____

_____

_____

_____

86. How does Matthew 16:24 apply here?

_____

_____

_____

87. During the battle with Authades, the dragon suddenly changed into another creature and Josiah recognized his adversary. What was he actually battling?

_____

_____

88. When the dragon was dead, Josiah found the Crown of Kuros. What did it look like?

❑ It was a small, crystalline crown with a base of pure gold.

❑ It was a large, golden crown set with jewels.

❑ It was a polished silver crown with glowing sapphires.

❑ It was a small, plain crown made of dark metal.

89. In just one sentence, give the message of *The Crown of Kuros*:

_____

_____

_____

90. **Thought question:** Is *your* heart surrendered to the King? Put a check mark where you would fit on the scale below.

Cold ☐ ☐ ☐ ☐ ☐ ☐ ☐ ☐ ☐ ☐ Hot

Now read Revelation 3:15, 16. **MEMORIZE** those two verses.

For further study: Rom. 12:1,2; I Cor. 5:14,15; Mark 12:28-33; John 14:15-25

JUST FOR FUN!

1. Choose a particular chapter (or scene) from the book and act it out with your class or with your family.

2. Make a crown for King Emmanuel to wear.

3. Create bows and arrows from sticks and string—hold a tournament! (Each participant would take a special name: Sir Humility, Lady Patience, etc.)

4. Put the song on page 60 to music.

5. Draw the members of the Council of Six on separate posters. At the bottom of each poster, describe that warlord's strategy to take over the kingdom.

6. Draw a picture of Prince Josiah battling the dragon Authades. (Remember that the battle takes place inside a cave.)

Book Five
The Dragon's Egg

This fifth book contains a somber warning for all believers: sin is deceptive and easily gets out of control. When Princess Gilda and Prince Selwyn refuse the offer of a gift forbidden by King Emmanuel, Prince Josiah accepts, not realizing the impact that his actions will have on the Castle of Faith. Too late he realizes that he is powerless to control the beast that he has unleashed upon Terrestria.

1. *The Dragon's Egg* opens with Prince Josiah and his two companions rescuing an elderly peasant couple from disaster. When they found the couple's cottage on fire, they:
- ❑ Saved the man from the fire.
- ❑ Saved the woman from the fire.
- ❑ Saved the cottage from being destroyed.
- ❑ Saved the peasant couple's only cow.

2. In order to show their gratitude, the elderly couple offered their rescuers their prize possession: a rare and beautiful egg. Who recognized it as a dragon's egg? _____

3. Describe the dragon's egg in just three words:

_____   _____   _____

4. Describe the emotions that Josiah experienced as he viewed the enormous egg:

_____

_____

_____

5. Why did Selwyn insist that they must not accept the egg from the peasant couple?

❑ He knew that it would be too heavy to carry.

❑ He knew that the other residents of the Castle of Faith would be jealous.

❑ He was afraid of being robbed on the way home to the castle.

❑ He knew that possession of the egg was forbidden by King Emmanuel.

6. Why did the peasant tell them that the egg could never hatch?

_____

_____

_____

7. On the ride back to the castle, Gilda confessed that she found herself wanting the egg even more when she learned that it was forbidden by King Emmanuel. What does her statement show us about human nature?

_____

_____

8. Do you ever find yourself wanting something, or wanting to do something, just because it is wrong?

_____

9. Jeremiah 17:9 tells us what three things about our own heart?

It is _____ _____ _____ _____.

It is _____ _____.

It cannot be _____.

10. Verse 10 tells us of someone who knows the human heart. Who is it?

_____

11. In Chapter 2, we find Prince Josiah in the southwest tower of the castle, wrestling with the desire to own the dragon's egg. What two things did he do to strengthen his own heart and give him victory over the temptation?

_____

_____

12. At the end of Chapter 2, Sir Faithful sent Prince Josiah on a special mission to the Castle of Steadfastness. Describe what Josiah was supposed to do:

_____

_____

13. When Josiah protested that he was too young for such an assignment, the castle steward replied that was exactly why he was sending him. What reason did he give for wanting to send a young person?

> "I am eternally grateful to Emmanuel, and I rejoice to serve him."
> —Prince Josiah

_____

14. When discussing the marquis with Josiah, Sir Faithful said, "Sometimes the heart wanders and love grows cold. When a child of Emmanuel loses the wonder of his or her adoption, he or she is capable of just about anything. Perhaps this is where we now find Sir Dither." What did he mean by these words?

_____

_____

_____

15. *True* or *False*   It is easy for the human heart to wander and for love to grow cold.

16. *True* or *False*   Children of the King who are busy serving him seldom wander.

17. *True* or *False*   There is no real way to keep our hearts from wandering.

18. As he went to the Castle of Steadfastness, Josiah worried about how the nobleman would respond when he tried to talk with him, and yet, an unusual incident drew the two together. Describe how Josiah met Sir Dither:

_____

_____

_____

19. As the prince and the marquis returned Sir Dither's falcon to its cage, Sir Dither confessed that he had lost heart and quit serving Emmanuel. What did he say had caused his love to grow cold? Put a check mark beside all that apply:

❑ He had paid a high price to serve the King.
❑ He had been influenced by the spellavision.
❑ He had been mocked for serving King Emmanuel.
❑ He had grown discouraged.
❑ He suffered from poor health and a lack of energy.

20. What did Josiah do that touched Sir Dither's heart and re-kindled his love for Emmanuel?

_____

_____

21. What did the marquis do to make sure that his heart would not be drawn away again?

_____

_____

60

22. As Josiah was riding back to the Castle of Faith, thanking his King for using him, he thought about the dragon's egg. He failed to realize the danger he was in when he told himself, "Surely a quick look _____ _____ _____ _____."

23. Why was this dangerous thinking?

_____

_____

_____

24. What happened when he went back for a "quick look"?

_____

_____

_____

25. **Thought question:** Did Josiah intend to take the egg when he went back for another look? _____ Give reasons for your answer:

_____

_____

_____

26. For discussion: Josiah was just coming from a victory at the Castle of Steadfastness. He had been instrumental in restoring Sir Dither to fellowship and service to his King. How do you suppose that he could now commit an act of direct disobedience to King Emmanuel?

27. When he returned to the Castle of Faith, where did he hide the dragon's egg?
    ❏ In the castle well
    ❏ In a hollow tree
    ❏ In a gooseberry thicket
    ❏ In a haystack

28. Supper in the great hall was always Prince Josiah's favorite time of the day, but on this occasion he did not enjoy the food, the music, or the fellowship. Why not?

_____

_____

29. In Psalm 51, as King David is repenting of his great sin of immorality and murder, he cries out, "Make me to hear joy and gladness; that the bones which thou hast broken may rejoice." What do you suppose David meant by those words?

_____

_____

_____

30. That night, alone in his solar, Josiah finds that he has no desire to send a petition to his King, as he normally did each evening. Why not?

_____

_____

_____

31. Look up Isaiah 59:2, which was written to God's people. What does it tell us about sin?

_____

_____

32. Prince Josiah had a dream that night about going to the Golden City and standing empty-handed before King Emmanuel. What do you suppose prompted the dream?

_____

_____

_____

62

33. At the end of Chapter 5, as Josiah went to the peasant's cottage to return the dragon's egg, he discovered that the cottage did not even exist. Was the cottage real, or did it merely exist in Josiah's imagination? Give reasons for your answer.

_____

_____

_____

34. Josiah left the egg in the clearing and rode away, yet turned back for one final look at the egg. Why was this a mistake?

> **"We must be faithful to guard our hearts so that we never find ourselves desiring that which our King has disallowed."**
> **–Prince Selwyn**

_____

_____

_____

35. Josiah spent most of Chapter 6 fighting two determined Little-kins for possession of the egg. In the end he apparently was victorious and took possession of the egg once again, but we are told that in reality he had walked into a clever trap. Describe what had just taken place:

_____

_____

_____

_____

36. When he took the dragon's egg into the Castle of Faith, where did Josiah hide it at first?
- ❏ In the castle well
- ❏ In the loft over the stables
- ❏ Behind the great hall
- ❏ In the garde-robe (bathroom)

37. After having the dream again of standing before the King, Josiah took the egg into the forest, determined to crush it and destroy it. Why did he not do it?

_____

_____

_____

38. Possession of the forbidden egg not only separated Josiah from fellowship with his King, but also from three other close friends. Name them: _____, _____, and

_____.

39. In Chapter 8, Josiah received a visit from Sir Dither of the Castle of Steadfastness, who gave him a very valuable gift. What was that gift, and what prompted the marquis to give it?

_____

_____

_____

40. Josiah experienced a sense of shame as Sir Dither told of how his heart had been changed by Josiah's words. Why did Josiah experience shame?

_____

_____

_____

41. At that moment, Josiah also made a sudden realization. What was it?

_____

_____

_____

42. At the chapter's conclusion, Prince Josiah made a horrendous discovery. What did he find?

_____

43. What emotions did Josiah experience as he made the discovery?

_____

_____

44. Did he search the castle from a sense of responsibility, or from fear that his disobedience would be discovered?

_____

_____

Give reasons for your answer:

_____

_____

_____

45. After Prince Josiah realized that the strange little creature in his solar was a hatchling dragon, he began to feed it, rather than destroy it. Why?

_____

_____

46. What does this teach us about the deceitfulness of sin?

_____

_____

47. What does God command us to do once we realize that we have let sin into our lives? _____ and _____ it.

48. **Thought question:** Can you think of an area in your own life where you are allowing wrong attitudes, thoughts, or actions to remain, rather than confessing and forsaking them?

49. **Thought question:** Can you think of any good reason that would keep you from confessing and forsaking those sins right now?

50. In Chapter 10, Josiah and Selwyn rode with the other knights to the defense of the Castle of Virtue. What assignment did Lord Watchful give to Captain Assurance and his garrison of knights?

_____

_____

51. What assignment did he give to Captain Diligence and his garrison?

_____

52. With which captain did Selwyn and Josiah ride?

_____

53. During the battle, an enemy horseman rode down upon Josiah at full gallop. When Josiah swung his mighty sword, what happened?

_____

_____

54. What happened to Josiah?

_____

Why? _____

_____

55. *True or False* Prince Josiah was nearly killed in the battle.

66

56. *True or False*   Selwyn saved Josiah's life.

57. *True or False*   Josiah sent a petition, but it landed in the dirt.

58. In the desperation of the battle, at a time when Josiah needed King Emmanuel's help the most, his petition never reached the throne room. Why not?

_____

_____

59. What does Psalm 66:18 say about this? Write out the verse:

_____

_____

60. **Thought question:** Does this mean that our King will not even listen to us when we refuse to deal with sin in our lives?

_____

_____

_____

61. What did Selwyn do to rescue Josiah?

_____

_____

_____

62. What were the results of Josiah possessing the forbidden egg? Put a check mark beside all that apply:
- ❑ He was ineffective and weak in battle.
- ❑ He jeopardized the lives of his fellow soldiers.
- ❑ He received wounds that left scars.
- ❑ He caused his garrison to lose the battle.
- ❑ His petitions were not answered.
- ❑ He lost his position as a son of King Emmanuel.

63. When the dragon first spoke to Josiah, the young prince expressed amazement that the creature could talk. The dragon replied, "I've been learning your language—your spoken language, and the language of your heart." What did the creature mean by that?

_____

_____

_____

64. In Chapter 11, we find Josiah making plans to destroy the dragon, even to the point that he puts the dragon into a large sack and takes him into the forest. Why did he not carry through on his plans?

_____

_____

65. **Thought question:** Josiah abandoned the dragon in the forest, yet the creature was waiting in his solar when he returned to the castle. How did the dragon know the way home?

_____

_____

66. **Thought question:** How is this like the power of sin?

_____

_____

67. In Chapter 12, Selwyn sighted the dragon. What was Josiah's response?

_____

_____

_____

68. In the same chapter, Sir Faithful reported to the castle residents that there had been sightings of a Cararian Greatwing dragon in

the vicinity of the castle, yet Josiah was not alarmed and seemed to take no responsibility for bringing this danger upon the castle residents. How should he have responded?

_____

_____

_____

69. How did Josiah respond when Sir Faithful warned the castle residents that a Cararian Greatwing was the fiercest of dragons and was capable of great destruction?

_____

_____

70. Why do you think that believers are often nonchalant about sin and the dangers that it poses?

_____

_____

71. How should Josiah have responded?

_____

_____

72. Chapter 12 closes as the dragon strikes a personal blow against Josiah. What great loss did Josiah suffer as the result of owning the dragon?

_____

_____

73. Do you think that this loss alerted Josiah that even greater danger was coming? _____ Should it have alerted him to that eventuality?

_____

74. In Chapter 13, the dragon attacked the Castle of Faith, once while Josiah was away, and once in his presence, and he witnessed for himself its tremendous power and animosity toward the residents of the castle, yet he determined to fight it alone. What caused him to reach that decision? Place an X beside the one wrong answer.
- ❑ He knew that only he could stop the dragon.
- ❑ He had fought a dragon before and been victorious.
- ❑ He had faith in the power of Emmanuel's sword.
- ❑ He wanted to protect his friends.

75. **Thought question:** Although Prince Josiah had witnessed the tremendous size and ferocious power of the dragon, he set out **ALONE** to fight it. Why did he not enlist help from his friends?

_____

_____

_____

76. In the solar, Josiah had seen the dragon display an unusual ability that should have told the young prince that the beast would be almost impossible to do battle with. What was that ability?

_____

_____

77. Describe the battle in the forest:

_____

_____

_____

_____

78. Josiah carried the invincible sword of King Emmanuel. Why was he defeated by the dragon?

_____

79. What kept him from being killed?

_____

80. The chapter closes as that which Josiah feared most took place. What was it?

_____

_____

81. What were the results of Josiah's disobedience? Mark all that apply.
- ❏ He was banished to his solar.
- ❏ He lost the privilege of dining in the great hall.
- ❏ His testimony within the castle was marred.
- ❏ He was shamed before his friends.
- ❏ He lost opportunities to serve the King.
- ❏ He brought dishonor upon the name of the King.
- ❏ He lost the joy of being the son of King Emmanuel.
- ❏ He missed the joy of participating in the King's Supper.

82. In Chapter 15, Prince Josiah left the Castle of Faith in the darkness of the night. What was his motivation for leaving?

_____

_____

83. Was he right to leave? _____

84. **Thought question:** Can you think of a better course of action that he should have taken?

_____

_____

_____

_____

_____

85. As Josiah stumbled through the darkness of the night, cold, tired, and lonely, he came upon a fire, a meal, and a sleeping pallet that had obviously been prepared for him. What is being portrayed here?

> "The longer you wait, my prince, the more difficult will be your task. The dragon grows larger and fiercer with every passing day." —Sir Wisdom

_____

_____

86. Sir Wisdom met Josiah at the campfire and told him the reason for his failure in attempting to destroy the dragon. What was it?

_____

_____

87. Would he have had victory if his motivation had been right?

_____

88. The nobleman told the young prince of four things that he must do to gain victory over the dragon. Name them:

1. _____

2. _____

3. _____

4. _____

89. Sir Wisdom asked Josiah to uproot a tiny sapling, which he did easily, and then to uproot a giant oak, which he could not do. What was the nobleman trying to illustrate?

_____

_____

90. While passing through a small city Josiah met a merchant who convinced him that the dragon could be trained and controlled. Was the merchant correct? _____
Why or why not?

_____

_____

91. The merchant taught Josiah to call the dragon by clapping six times. What is the significance of the number six as used in the Bible?

_____

_____

92. In the presence of the merchant, the great dragon followed every command of Josiah's perfectly. What was happening here?

_____

_____

93. In the same scene we find Josiah deciding to give the dragon a name. This gives us a clue as to what was going on in Josiah's mind. Why did he decide to name the dragon?

_____

_____

94. In Chapter 17, Josiah's disobedience brought tragedy to an innocent bystander. What happened?

_____

_____

95. How did Josiah realize that the dragon was not under his control?

_____

_____

96. **Thought question:** Many times we deceive ourselves, much as Josiah was doing, into thinking that we can accommodate sin in our lives and yet have it under our control. Why is this dangerous thinking?

_____

_____

_____

97. According to James 1, sin, when it is finished, bringeth forth

_____.

98. In Chapter 18, we find Prince Josiah in a place he had vowed that he would never go. Where was it?

_____

_____

99. Josiah told Sir Faithful that it had been just a short while since he had battled the dragon Authades and surrendered his heart to King Emmanuel. He then asked, "How could I have done such a thing as hatching the dragon's egg? Why is my heart no longer yielded?" What was the steward's answer?

_____

_____

_____

_____

100. The castle steward instructed Josiah to go to the Castle of Knowledge and study his book in order to prepare himself for the battle with the dragon. On the way to the castle Josiah ran into an old foe from days past. Who was it?

_____

_____

101. Name two things that this foe told Josiah in order to discourage him:

1. _____

2. _____

102. At the end of the chapter, Josiah was captured by another foe from days gone by. Who was it?

_____

103. At the conclusion of Book 4, *The Crown of Kuros*, we see Josiah as a victorious young prince, heart yielded to his king, and happy to be in his service—yet, at this point in the story, we find Josiah defeated, unable to control the dragon that he has unleashed upon the kingdom. What steps had he taken to reach that point? Number the following in chronological order:

___ He and his friends helped a couple in an emergency.

___ They were offered the egg of a dragon.

___ Together, they refused.

___ He held the egg.

___ The egg hatched.

___ He hid the egg in his solar.

___ He hid the egg in the forest.

___ The merchant taught him to "control" the dragon.

___ He accepted the egg as a gift.

___ He took the egg to the forest, but couldn't crush it.

___ Josiah went back for another look at the egg.

___ He took the dragon to the forest, but couldn't kill it.

___ He hid the egg in the stables.

___ Josiah tracked the dragon to the forest.

___ The dragon killed his falcon.

___ The dragon attacked the castle.

___ Josiah left the village and was captured by the Giant of Fear.

___ Josiah found himself in the Village of Indifference.

___ The dragon killed the goatherd's son.

104. In Chapter 19, Josiah visited the Castle of Knowledge and experienced what Biblical scene in order to learn to defeat the dragon?

_____

105. In Chapter 20, Josiah battled the dragon. What happened?

_____

_____

_____

_____

106. How can you guard your heart against the "dragons" that would draw you away from your King?

_____

_____

For further study: Joshua 7:1-26; Isa. 59: 2, 12-15; Rom. 5:12-21; Rom. 7:6-25

MEMORIZE: James 1:12-15

JUST FOR FUN:

1. Act out the scene from the peasant's cottage. Have a very forceful, domineering person play the part of the peasant. (This person refuses to take "no" for an answer.) Afterward, talk about peer pressure and how to resist temptation.

2. Discuss how yielding to temptation can hurt someone or even something that we really love. (Example: Thunder the dragon killing Lightning the hawk.)

3. Discuss how a "harmless" infraction of the law can have devastating consequences. (For example, running a stop sign and perhaps killing a child, etc.)

4. Using a hen's egg, act out the scene where Josiah takes the dragon's egg to the forest but cannot bring himself to crush it. Discuss the reasons why he failed.

5. Give an egg to each person and have them write the name of a specific sin over which they cannot seem to get victory. Talk about ways to achieve victory and then crush each egg.

6. Using modeling clay, make Thunder the dragon as you think he would look.

Book Six
The Golden Lamps

This sixth book in the Terrestria Chronicles tells the story of Hazah, a sleepy little village in the kingdom of Terrestria. When the village is attacked by Argamor's forces, the villagers petition King Emmanuel to build them a castle for protection. Their King responds by sending a master engineer and trained craftsmen to assist the town in the building of their own castle. All goes well until the workers begin discovering mysterious golden lamps that have the power to jeopardize the project.

The Golden Lamps challenges readers young and old alike to make certain that the King's business is always the priority in their lives.

1. The Prologue describes a mysterious figure making golden lamps at a burning forge deep within a mountain. Who was the mysterious craftsman, and what was the purpose of the lamps?

_____

_____

2. After making the lamps, the craftsman challenges them to help him capture "the one golden object that rightfully belongs to me." What was that golden object that he was striving so hard to obtain? (The battle for Terrestria is a battle for this object.)

_____

3. Chapter 1 opens with young knights-in-training skirmishing under the direction of a tall woodsman by the name of Paul. The author does not provide much detail about this man, yet a lot can

78

be learned by observing him. Name four things that you know about Paul:

(1) _____

(2) _____

(3) _____

(4) _____

4. As we watch Paul's interaction with the young men of the village, we realize that their training in knighthood was extremely important to him. Why was he so determined that they receive proper training?

> **"They have placed personal gain above service to their King, though the gain they seek is worthless in the next life."**
> **— Encouragement**

_____

_____

5. Paul's interaction with the crockery merchant, Demas, showed that service to the King was not of great importance to Demas. What was the merchant's passion?

_____

6. What reason did Demas give for rejecting Phillip as a possible son-in-law?

_____

_____

7. Was Demas correct in his negative assessment of Phillip? _____ Give reasons to support your answer.

_____

_____

_____

8. As Chapter 1 closes, what was about to happen in the village of Hazah?

_____

_____

9. Describe the attack on the village:

_____

_____

_____

_____

10. As the attackers rode from the village, one dark knight seized a little girl and rode away with her. Who saved her life? _____ Whose daughter was the little girl? _____ _____

11. After the village reeve resigned, the townspeople chose Paul as the new reeve. Paul told the people that in order to protect their village they needed to petition the King for what?_____

12. As the townspeople discussed the need for a castle, who opposed the idea? _____

13. When the townspeople petitioned King Emmanuel to build them a castle, how did he respond?

_____

_____

_____

_____

> **"They have forgotten that service to their King brings rewards that will follow them all the way to the Golden City."**
> **—Encouragement**

14. What was the castle a picture of?

_____

15. How much of the villagers' time did the construction plan call for?

_____

_____

16. Where would the materials for the castle come from?

_____

_____

17. In Chapter 4, as James and his staff are helping the villagers select the site for the castle, which of the following was NOT a consideration?
 ❑ It had to be close to the river.
 ❑ It had to be in a sunny location.
 ❑ It had to be close to the present location of the village.
 ❑ It had to be easily defended.

18. What location was finally selected?

_____

_____

19. When Demas suggested a location close to the present village, James told him why the site was unsuitable. What did James tell him?

_____

_____

_____

20. What work assignment was Demas given?

_____

21. What work assignment was Phillip given?

_____

What was his work assignment changed to?

_____

22. How did the work assignments of these two men lead to animosity on Demas' part?

_____

_____

23. As Phillip showed Rebecca the layout for the new castle, she asked why the inner curtain wall would be so much taller than the outer curtain. What did Phillip tell her?

_____

_____

24. What was to be the main purpose of the castle?

_____

25. Why was the castle project so important to the town of Hazah?

_____

_____

_____

26. Before the project was even started, James of Arwyn warned the villagers of what?

_____

_____

_____

27. What name was chosen for the new castle?

_____

82

28. What was the name of the village changed to?

_____

Why was the name changed?

_____

29. When the work on the castle actually began, how did the villagers respond?
- ❑ They worked willingly and did more than was required.
- ❑ They worked grudgingly and complained frequently.
- ❑ They were excited at first but lost interest after the first day.
- ❑ Some worked willingly; others refused to work.

30. When Phillip was injured while cutting down a tree, the fore-man of the lumbering crew realized what had caused the accident. What did he see?

_____

_____

31. Who was opposed to the building of the castle?

_____

32. Opposition often arises when we do the Lord's work. Name the two main sources of the opposition:

_____

_____

33. In Chapter 5, the saboteur struck again. What did he do?

_____

_____

34. Why did he do such minimal damage?

_____

_____

35. What steps were taken to protect the project against further interference?

_____

_____

36. The chapter closes as Demas bans Phillip from his home and forbids him to see Rebecca. What brought about such hostility?

_____

_____

37. In Chapter 6, Phillip encountered a quarry such as he had never seen before. Describe the animal:

_____

_____

38. What was unusual about the animal?

_____

_____

_____

_____

_____

39. What happened when Phillip pursued it?

_____

_____

> "But when a man sets goals that are beyond his reach and then becomes consumed with reaching them, those goals become his master and he becomes their slave."
> —Paul the woodsman

_____

40. What did he find when he took his horse back to retrieve the carcass?

_____

_____

41. After checking the scene, what did he decide had happened?

_____

_____

42. Describe the third attack of the saboteur:

_____

_____

_____

43. When two young workers saw a man that was possibly the saboteur, who did they identify the person as?

_____

44. What was Demas' response when confronted?

_____

_____

45. Who stood up for Demas and exonerated him?

_____

46. How did Demas respond?

_____

_____

_____

_____

47. As Demas and the other quarrymen were working in the quarry, a wall of rock fell away. What did Demas find as a result?

_____

_____

48. Moments after Demas made his spectacular find, an old man appeared with a sobering warning. What did he advise Demas to do?

_____

49. "The power of the lamp can be used for good or evil," the old man warned. What did he mean by these words?

_____

_____

50. What special power did the lamp possess?

_____

_____

51. "Even if you use it for good, the lamp will seek to possess you," the stranger then warned. Why did he say this?

_____

_____

_____

52. What warning does the Bible gives us in I Timothy 6: 6-10?

_____

_____

_____

53. The Bible does not say that "money is the root of all evil", as many people think. What *does* it say is the root of all evil?

_____

54. **Thought question:** How should we as believers view money?

_____

_____

86

55. **Thought question:** Money is a necessary part of life, yet seeking it brings certain dangers. What are those dangers?

_____

_____

_____

56. **Thought question:** How can we guard our hearts against the dangers that Sir Wisdom warned about?

_____

_____

_____

57. As Chapter 9 opens, the power of the lamp begins to reveal itself. What happened to Demas as the result of finding the lamp?

_____

_____

58. What happened when Demas tried to sell the golden lamp?

_____

_____

_____

Why?

_____

_____

59. Demas told Paul that he no longer had time to work on the castle. What had happened to his heart?

_____

_____

60. **Thought question:** How much of Demas' attitude toward the castle was the result of the golden lamp? How much was the outworking of his own selfishness?

_____

_____

_____

61. When Paul pointed out that the proposed site of Demas' new home was too far from the castle, why was Demas not concerned?

_____

62. Why did Paul refuse Demas' offer of a partnership and the wealth that would have resulted?

_____

_____

63. What does this show us about Paul's character?

_____

_____

64. Chapter 9 closes as a second villager finds a golden lamp at the quarry. Imagine that you are that villager. Describe how you found that lamp and what your initial reactions were:

_____

_____

_____

65. In Chapter 10, we find that James of Arwyn was very discouraged. What was the reason for his discouragement?

_____

_____

66. What did Encouragement use to lift the engineer's spirits?

_____

88

67. At this point in the story, how many lamps had been found?

_____

68. How did they affect the building of the castle?

_____

_____

69. **Thought question:** Why does wealth tend to affect people in this way?

_____

_____

70. In Book 4, at the council of war in Lower Terrestria, what did Captain Covetous plan to use to draw people's hearts away from their King?

_____

_____

71. Although work on the castle had nearly come to a standstill, why did the minstrel say that James had not failed in his service to King Emmanuel?

_____

_____

_____

72. What did he offer as a possible solution to the problem of apathy toward the castle project?

_____

_____

73. In Chapter 11, as Prince Josiah tells the story of his battle with the dragon Authades, what is revealed of his character? Check all that apply.

☐ He was candid and honest about his failures.
☐ He admitted his own selfishness.
☐ He was willing to learn from his mistakes.
☐ He was courageous.
☐ He was confident in his own abilities.
☐ He was determined to battle the dragon in his own strength.
☐ His purpose in telling the story was to help the young squires.
☐ His desire was to surrender his heart to the King.

74. What does this chapter reveal of the relationship between Josiah and Princess Gilda?

_____

_____

75. In Chapter 12, we find Phillip hunting the golden hart. How did the animal escape?

_____

_____

76. The chapter ends as a young man identifying himself as Phillip the huntsman showed Prince Josiah a burned-out castle, telling him that the Castle of Hope had been destroyed. Who was the young man? _____ What castle did Josiah see? _____

77. What was this person's purpose in deceiving the young prince?

_____

_____

78. When Josiah addressed the villagers, upon whom was he depending for guidance? _____

79. Of what two truths did Josiah remind the villagers?

1. _____

2. _____

80. What was the response of the villagers?

_____

_____

81. As Josiah talked with individual villagers, what excuses did they give for seeking golden lamps instead of working on the King's castle?

The tall farmer: "I'm doing this _____ ____ _____."

The young couple: "We have _____ _____ _____

_____."

Barnabas: "My family and I _____ _____ _____."

The mortar mixer: "My wife has _____ _____ ____."

82. When Josiah realized that his words had had no effect on the villagers as individuals or as a group, what did he decide to do?

_____

_____

_____

83. Chapter 15 closes as Prince Josiah receives a visit from Lady Prudence. What did she instruct him to do?

_____

_____

84. How did the men of Mitspah reach the Lake of Destiny?

_____

_____

85. On the first visit to the lake, what did the men see?

_____

_____

86. What was the outcome of the battle that they witnessed?

_____

_____

_____

87. How did the visit to the future affect the men?

_____

_____

88. *True or False* After witnessing a victory as a result of the completed castle, the men of Mitspah were eager to return to the present and complete the castle.

89. *True or False* The first visit to the Lake of Destiny seemed to have little effect on the men of Mitspah.

90. In Chapter 17, Josiah and the men of Mitspah made a second visit to the future through the Lake of Destiny. What was different about the second visit?

> **"Excellence for the sake of excellence often becomes a matter of pride; and pride never glorifies the King."**
> **–Sir Wisdom**

_____

_____

91. Describe the second battle that they witnessed:

_____

_____

_____

92. What was the effect upon the men?

_____

_____

93. In Chapter 18, Josiah accompanied Phillip on a hunt and they came upon the golden hart that the young huntsman had sought so fervently. As Phillip prepared to shoot, who stopped him?

_____

94. According to Sir Wisdom, what was the reason that Phillip had pursued the golden hart so relentlessly?

_____

95. What did the golden hart represent?

_____

_____

96. Sir Wisdom told Phillip that Argamor had distracted him from his service to the King. Explain what he meant:

_____

_____

97. **Thought question:** Is it possible for a child of the King to become so enamored with serving the King that he forgets the King Himself? _____ Explain your answer:

_____

_____

_____

98. **Thought question:** At what point does the quest for excellence become a matter of pride?

_____

_____

_____

99. **Thought question:** In your opinion, which is worse? (1) Slipshod, half-hearted service to the King (which is sin), or (2) Excellence in service to the point that it becomes a matter of pride (which also is sin).

_____

_____

Explain your answer: _____

_____

100. The chapter closes as the castle saboteur is discovered. Who did it turn out to be? _____

101. The last chapter of _The Golden Lamps_ describes the battle for Mitspah. Who won the battle?

_____

Why?_____

_____

102. Two of the villagers did not survive the battle. Who were they?

_____

94

103. **Thought question:** Demas the crockery merchant put his own interests ahead of the King's work. What did it cost him?

_____

_____

104. Read Genesis 13 and 19. In what ways was Lot like Demas?

_____

_____

_____

105. What did the wrong decisions cost Lot?

_____

_____

_____

106. Where does the name "Demas" come from?

_____

_____

107. What is this Bible character known for?

_____

_____

_____

For further study: Psalm 37:1-5, 16-28; James 5:1-5; Eccles. 2:1-26; Matt. 19:16-29; Luke 12:13-31; Mark 10:17-30; Mark 4:19

MEMORIZE: I Timothy 6:6-12

JUST FOR FUN!

1. Wrap 13 salt shakers in gold foil or spray-paint them gold, then bury them in a sand-box—your own "quarry". Ask the students to help you build a wall, but tell them that they may dig for the "golden lamps" whenever they want to. Announce that anyone finding a lamp will receive a small prize. At the end of the activity, award some small prizes to those with salt shakers and even larger prizes to those who worked on the wall. Discuss the value of eternal things.

2. On another occasion, plan a "treasure hunt". Scatter small, wrapped candy in the yard and then place a large, empty package from some treat in a tree (perhaps 8-10 feet from the ground). As the children gather the candy, at least one child will decide to climb the tree to get the larger prize and will then discover that it is empty. After the hunt, discuss how Satan offers us things that look better than what God has given us. Point out that the devil's promises are empty.

3. Have each student or family member write out a petition to send to King Emmanuel. This can be a current need or a praise.

4. Create your own knight's protective armor and practice fighting for your King.

5. Using hot glue, small stones, matchsticks and Popsicle® sticks, build a model of the Castle of Hope. (This project will not be completed in one session.)

6. Plan for an adult to "sabotage" a small section of the project so that the young people experience the frustration that James of Arwyn and the villagers felt.

7. Have each student draw a picture of a peasant (male or female), and then draw that same person as royalty. For authenticity, consult an encyclopedia for pictures of medieval dress. Discuss what happens when a sinner becomes a child of God.

8. Beneath the pictures of the peasant-turned-royalty, have each student list the differences in the two "classes" of people. What differences would there be in their dress? Their speech? Their diet? (Compare the intake of physical food with the intake of food for the mind and soul.) What differences would there be in their future?

Book Seven
The Great War

In this final episode of the Terrestria Chronicles, King Emmanuel returns from the Golden City of the Redeemed!

Throughout the eons of time, Terrestria has been at war. Argamor and his dark forces are still determined to wrest control of the kingdom from the hands of King Emmanuel. Argamor's evil plans include Princess Gilda—her captivity is sure to result in the defeat of Prince Josiah and the downfall of the Castle of Faith. Just when it seems that the evil armies are about to win the final battle for Terrestria, His Majesty returns on a white horse.

The Great War gives the reader a behind-the-scenes look at the "shining ones"—the angelic ranks at work on our behalf today. In a fast-paced, panoramic overview of the book of Revelation, the reader catches just a glimpse of the almighty power of King Emmanuel and of the wondrous future that awaits in the Golden City of the Redeemed. The children of the King are encouraged to faithfully send petitions and watch for their King's return.

1. The book opens with a scene involving three "shining warriors" with shimmering wings and swift swords. Who are these powerful warriors?

_____

_____

2. One of the shining ones, a young warrior by the name of Olympas, had just been sent to Terrestria. What duty was he assigned?

_____

_____

98

3. What did Olympas do to demonstrate to the Captain his prowess with a sword?

_____

_____

4. Why was Tertius being assigned the command of another castle?

_____

_____

5. Olympas and Tertius are Roman names. Where do we find these names in Scripture? (Use your concordance.)

_____

6. Tertius and the Captain briefed Olympas on the state of affairs in the kingdom. Which of the following statements were true about Terrestria?
- ❑ There was an element of apathy among the King's children.
- ❑ Most of them rarely sent petitions to their King.
- ❑ Those who did seemed to send them from a sense of duty.
- ❑ The kingdom was weakened.
- ❑ Argamor's forces were slowly taking over.
- ❑ The Royal Ones were becoming like the peasants around them.
- ❑ They had forgotten that their King was coming back for them.

7. From their vantage atop the mountain, the three shining warriors observed one of the King's children sending a petition. Who was it?

_____

8. Tertius told Olympas, "That prince (Josiah) is your main source of power for the defense of the castle." What did he mean?

_____

_____

9. Olympas asked the Captain, "If the Royal Ones know about us, why should they not see us?" What did the Captain tell him?

_____

_____

_____

10. Olympas observed that that particular region of Terrestria had many castles and surmised that the kingdom should be safe. The Captain replied that many of the castles belonged to Argamor. What did he mean?

> **"The final battle of the Great War is about to commence, yet the King's children live as if they are totally unaware of what is happening."**
> **–The Captain**

_____

_____

_____

11. As the Captain left, what was the one thing he stressed to Olympas?

_____

_____

_____

12. His parting comment was, "Without _____, the Castle of Faith will be lost."

13. The chapter closes as an assailant is preparing an attack upon Prince Josiah. Who was that assailant?

_____

14. In Chapter 2 we meet Ethan, the three-year-old son of Prince Josiah and Princess Gilda. Describe this little boy in three words:

1. _____
2. _____
3. _____

15. What was Josiah's nickname for his son?

_____

16. What was Ethan's greatest desire?

_____

_____

17. In Chapter 3, Josiah and Selwyn settled a dispute over the use of a river crossing and then were invited to a villager's home for supper. As they rode through town, what did the reeve ask them not to do?

_____

_____

18. The village magistrate had issued a decree that Emmanuel's coat of arms was not to be displayed within the village. Did he have the right to make that decree? _____ Why or why not?

_____

_____

19. Selwyn told the magistrate that Emmanuel's coat of arms was already on display in the village. To what was he referring?

_____

_____

20. Upon reaching home, Josiah found that his son Ethan had developed what type of an illness?

_____

21. Selwyn asked Sir Faithful how Terrestria could have reached the point where His Majesty's coat of arms would be prohibited. What was the steward's reply?

_____

_____

_____

22. The chapter closes as Prince Josiah sent a desperate petition for what type of an emergency?

_____

_____

23. Chapter 5 opens as Josiah spends an entire night in the northwest tower sending petitions for the life of his son. What was Ethan's condition the next morning?

_____

_____

24. Josiah was so delighted with Ethan's apparent recovery that he had what made to celebrate?
- ❑ A child-size sword
- ❑ A doublet and cloak
- ❑ An elaborate cake
- ❑ A banner with Emmanuel's coat of arms

25. Selwyn and Josiah were sent to the Castle of Diligence. What was their mission?

_____

_____

26. As they reached the castle they discovered that it was under assault. How did they respond?

_____

_____

27. A garrison of shining warriors was present to defend the castle. As the attack got underway, why were they powerless to act?

_____

_____

28. As the two young princes rode to the defense of the castle, Josiah realized that there was a much more effective way to aid the castle defenders. What was it?

_____

_____

29. What happened when they began to send petitions?

_____

_____

30. What was the outcome of the battle?

_____

31. When Josiah returned to the Castle of Faith, he learned that he and Gilda had just suffered an incredible loss. What was it?

_____

_____

32. In the midst of his grief, Josiah found a remarkable item on the floor of the solar. What was it?

_____

_____

33. What was the blossom a token of?

_____

_____

34. What happened to Ethan's miniature sword?

_____

35. At the burial, how did Josiah suddenly find peace?

_____

_____

36. Josiah's heart was in turmoil as he realized that King Emmanuel had miraculously answered one of his petitions but apparently not answered another. What were the two petitions?

The first: _____

The second: _____

37. **Thought question:** Why did Emmanuel answer Josiah's two petitions on behalf of the castle but not the many ones he sent for the life of his son?

_____

_____

_____

_____

38. Have you (or your family) ever prayed for something that seemed that it was in accord with God's will, and yet not see Him answer as you thought He should? Talk about it.

39. As Chapter 6 continues we find that both Gilda and Josiah struggle with Ethan's death. Describe the differences in their responses. Josiah's response:

_____

_____

_____

Gilda's response:

_____

_____

_____

40. As Josiah was in the northwest tower with Sir Faithful, the clouds parted to reveal what?

_____

_____

"Your King can be trusted. His plans for you may at times include periods of darkness, and periods of pain."
–Sir Faithful

_____

_____

41. What was the significance of the constellation that Josiah saw above the castle?

_____

_____

_____

42. What did the darkness of the night allow Josiah to do that he could not do during the day?

_____

_____

43. Thought question: Why does our King allow dark periods to come into our lives?

_____

_____

_____

_____

44. How did Josiah relate to the words of the minstrel's song?

_____

_____

45. After hearing the song, what decision did he make?

_____

_____

46. Chapter 7 opens as Josiah reads a letter from Gilda. What did the letter say?

_____

_____

_____

_____

47. When Josiah showed Gilda's letter to Sir Faithful, what did the steward advise him to do?

_____

_____

48. When Princess Gilda and her lady-in-waiting stopped at an inn for a break from their ride, whom did they meet?

_____

_____

49. What does the word *acrimonious* mean?

_____

_____

50. As Selwyn and Josiah were tracking Gilda and Miriam, they came across a valley that was the scene of some very alarming activity. What did they see?

_____

_____

51. Fill in the blanks in the statement that Sir Faithful made when discussing Gilda: "_____ is a terrible _____ in the hands of our adversary."

> **"But during the darkest of times, if you'll look up, you can see the shepherd."**
> **–Sir Faithful**

52. What can bitterness do to a child of the King?

_____

_____

_____

_____

53. Which of the following can bitterness <u>not</u> do to a child of the King?

❑ Take away the joy of being a child of the King.

❑ Take away the right to be a child of the King.

❑ Cause you to be ineffective in service to the King

❑ Dampen your desire to serve the King.

❑ Drive unbelievers away from the King.

54. Even though Gilda was bitter at the loss of her son, when Lady Acrimonious attacked the character of King Emmanuel, Gilda defended Him. Why do you suppose that she did?

_____

_____

_____

55. Where did Mara (Lady Acrimonious) take Gilda?

_____

56. The chapter closes as Mara discloses to the knight on the stairs just why Gilda's capture was so important to Argamor and his evil forces. What was the plan?

_____

_____

57. In Chapter 9, Prince Josiah and Prince Selwyn battled a mass of deadly brambles intent on destroying them. What do the brambles represent?

_____

_____

58. In Chapter 10, when Josiah and Selwyn found the Bramble Castle, why did Selwyn turn back to the Castle of Faith?

_____

Why did Josiah insist on entering the castle?

_____

_____

59. How did Josiah raise the portcullis and open the gates of the Bramble Castle?

_____

108

60. As Josiah was exploring the Bramble Castle he came upon a huge knight and did battle with him, yet found that he was nothing more than an empty suit of armor. What does the empty knight represent?

_____

_____

61. Who actually accomplished the victory over the huge dark knight? _____

62. In Chapter 11, as Josiah returned from a fruitless search of the Bramble Castle, Sir Wisdom met him at a campfire with a hot meal to encourage him. Why was Josiah discouraged?
- ❑ He had lost Ethan.
- ❑ He had lost Gilda to bitterness.
- ❑ It seemed that King Emmanuel would never return from the Golden City.
- ❑ Dark forces were gathering near the Castle of Faith.

63. When the nobleman revealed Argamor's plans for Gilda, Josiah asked what he should do. What was Sir Wisdom's two-fold answer?
1. _____

2. _____

64. "I'm not certain that my petitions are doing any good," Josiah told Sir Wisdom. What caused him to say this?

_____

_____

65. Why did Sir Wisdom take the young prince to the Castle of Knowledge?

_____

_____

66. Which book did they visit in the Library of Learning?

_____

67. What book of the Bible does this represent?

_____

68. In Chapter 13, Josiah saw four fierce horsemen. Tell the color of each horse, tell what each rider was carrying, and then tell what each rider brought to the inhabitants of Terrestria:

(1) The _____ horse: _____
Brought: _____

(2) The _____ horse: _____
Brought: _____

(3) The _____ horse: _____
Brought: _____

(4) The _____ horse: _____
Brought: _____

69. In the Book of Revelation, which rider was not actually carrying something?

_____

70. Sir Wisdom told Josiah that the appearance of the white horse signified that the time of judgment had come. Of what great judgment was he speaking?

_____

_____

How long will this period of judgment be upon Earth?

_____

Where do we find this period of judgment in the Bible?

_____

71. As the first four seals were opened in the Golden City, the first four riders appeared to bring judgment. What happened when the fifth seal was opened? (Revelation 6:9-11)

_____

_____

72. What happened when the sixth seal was opened? (Revelation 6:12-17)

_____

_____

73. How many seals were opened in all? _____

74. How many trumpets of judgment sounded when the seventh seal was opened? _____

75. Draw a line from each trumpet to the judgment that resulted. (See Revelation 8, 9.)

First trumpet   Waters poisoned

Second trumpet   Vials of judgment emptied

Third trumpet   Seas became blood

Fourth trumpet   Hailstones with fire

Fifth trumpet   Darkness one-third of the day

Sixth trumpet   Locusts torment people

Seventh trumpet   One-third of all people killed

76. How many vials (vessels) of judgment were poured out upon the earth? (See Revelation 16.)

_____

77. What was the name of the False King that Argamor set in place?

_____

78. What is the significance of that name and why was it chosen? (See Revelation 1:8.)

_____

_____

79. What is the special mark that the False King will compel all Terrestrians to receive?

_____

_____

_____

80. Chapter 14 closes as millions of warriors assembled on a great battlefield. What battle was about to take place?

_____

_____

_____

"This will be a battle like no other. You are about to witness the wrath and power of the King of kings!"
–Sir Wisdom

81. What happened to the vast armies assembled to do battle with King Emmanuel?

_____

_____

82. What happened to Argamor?

_____

_____

83. In Chapter 15, Sir Wisdom and Prince Josiah visited the future and experienced the thousand-year reign of King Emmanuel.

Josiah was amazed at the changes that had taken place. Name three of the amazing things that he observed:

1. _____

2. _____

3. _____

84. In Chapter 16, Josiah learned that Argamor was to be imprisoned during the thousand reign of Emmanuel. What would happen when Argamor would be released at the end of the thousand years?

_____

_____

_____

85. Describe the great judgment day, or "trial of the ages."

_____

_____

_____

86. In Chapter 17, why did Josiah and Selwyn go to the Valley of Discouragement?

_____

_____

_____

87. **Thought question:** Why do you suppose that they needed the ring to rescue Gilda?

_____

_____

_____

88. When Josiah and Selwyn entered the tower in the Castle of Bitterness, whom did they find in the solar with Gilda?

_____

89. Describe the scene as Selwyn and Josiah worked together to free Gilda:

_____

_____

_____

_____

90. When Selwyn and Josiah returned to the Castle of Faith with Gilda, what did they find?

_____

_____

91. How did they get into the castle?

_____

_____

92. What happened in the battle for the castle?

_____

_____

_____

93. Tell how the King's children left the Castle of Faith.

_____

_____

_____

94. Where in Scripture do we find the promise of our Lord's return?

_____

_____

95. What can we do to be prepared for His return?

_____

_____

96. **Thought question:** Why were Josiah's petitions so vital to the Castle of Faith?

_____

_____

_____

97. **Thought question:** Name some ways that our adversary attempts to keep us from sending petitions to our King:

_____

_____

_____

98. Using just five words, describe the Golden City of the Redeemed.

1. _____

2. _____

3. _____

4. _____

5. _____

99. Read Revelation 21 and 22. Write a brief description of heaven and of the New Jerusalem.

_____

_____

_____

_____

100. Whom did Josiah meet in the Golden City?

_____

101. What are the two main themes of *The Great War*?

(1) _____

(2) _____

For further study: I Cor. 15:51-58; Rev. 5-9; Rev. 16; Rev. 19-22

MEMORIZE: I Thessalonians 4:13-18

116

JUST FOR FUN!

1. The minstrel's song in Chapter 6 was written by twelve-year-old Zachary Cox. Compose your own poem as a tribute to your King. Some possible topics might be:

- The joy you experienced when the King adopted you into His family

- A petition to King Emmanuel urging him to return from the Golden City

- What it will be like when the King does return

- A song of praise that could be sung on the King's coronation day

2. Make two shields with King Emmanuel's coat of arms. Have students re-enact the scene where Josiah and Selwyn are ordered to lower their shields. Discuss how this is happening in society today. How should we respond?

3. Draw pictures of various scenes from the Apocalypse, perhaps even putting these together to form a visualized time line of the book.

4. Draw pictures of what life will be like after King Emmanuel comes back.

5. Designate one person to play the part of King Emmanuel, and have other students send petitions to him with various requests. (Privately instruct the "king" to answer certain petitions with a "yes" and others with a "no".) Discuss the question: Why did King Emmanuel answer Josiah's petitions on behalf of the Castle of Diligence, but apparently refuse to answer his petitions on behalf of his son, Ethan? Why does God answer some of our petitions with a "yes" while others are answered with a "no"?

6. Designate three young people to play Josiah, Gilda, and Selwyn as they enter the Golden City of the Redeemed. What will they see? What will they experience?